FRANCHISING IN INDONESIA 2014

Legal and Business Considerations

AF873374

KENDAL H. TYRE, JR., EXECUTIVE EDITOR
DIANA VILMENAY-HAMMOND, MANAGING EDITOR
PIERCE HAESUNG HAN, ASSISTANT EDITOR

LEXNOIR FOUNDATION

FOURTH QUARTER 2014

LexNoir Foundation is the charitable, educational arm of LexNoir, an international network of lawyers connecting the African Diaspora.

This publication, *Franchising in Indonesia 2014: Legal and Business Considerations*, contains excerpts from *Franchising in Asia 2014: Legal and Business Considerations*. Both works are published by LexNoir Foundation and reflect the points of view of the authors and editors as of the date of publication and do not necessarily represent the opinions, interpretations, or positions of the law firms or organizations with which they are affiliated, nor the opinions, interpretations or positions of LexNoir Foundation or LexNoir.

Nothing contained in this book is to be considered as the rendering of legal advice, either generally or in connection with any specific issues or case. Readers are responsible for obtaining advice from their own legal counsel or other professional. This book, any forms and agreements or other information herein are intended for educational and informational purposes only.

© 2014 LexNoir Foundation. All rights reserved.

www.lexnoir.org

Table of Contents

Page

Bibliography of International Franchise Resources

Kendal H. Tyre, Jr., Diana Vilmenay-Hammond, Pierce Haesung Han and Keri McWilliams
Nixon Peabody LLP

Acknowledgment

This book could not have been written without the hard work and dedication of each of the contributing authors and editors. Thank you.

We would like to acknowledge and extend our heartfelt gratitude to Maria Stallings of the Washington, D.C. office of Nixon Peabody LLP for her invaluable assistance in revising, proofing, and editing this publication.

About the Editors and Authors

Kendal H. Tyre, Jr. – Kendal is a partner in the Washington, D.C. office of Nixon Peabody LLP. He handles domestic and cross-border transactions, including mergers and acquisitions, joint ventures, strategic alliances, licensing, and franchise matters.

In his franchise and licensing practice, Kendal counsels domestic and international franchisors, franchisees, licensors, licensees and distributors regarding U.S. state and federal franchise laws as well as foreign franchise legislation in a variety of jurisdictions. Kendal drafts and provides advice with regard to franchise and license agreements and disclosure documents and has extensive experience drafting and negotiating a variety of other commercial agreements.

Kendal is a frequent contributor to franchise publications and a frequent speaker at franchise programs held by the American Bar Association Forum on Franchising and the International Franchise Association.

Kendal is co-chair of the firm's Diversity Action Committee and its Africa Group. Kendal is also the executive director of LexNoir Foundation.

E-mail address: ktyre@nixonpeabody.com

Diana Vilmenay-Hammond – Diana is an attorney in the Washington, D.C. office of Nixon Peabody LLP. She is a member of the firm's Franchise & Distribution team.

In her franchise practice, Diana works with domestic and international franchisors on transactional and litigation matters. Specifically, she counsels franchisor clients regarding state and federal franchise laws, disclosure and registration obligations. Diana drafts and negotiates various commercial agreements, including international franchise and development agreements.

Diana has co-authored numerous articles on franchising and frequently co-hosted the Nixon Peabody franchise law webinar series. Topics have included:

- "Franchise Case Law Round-Up: Implications for Your Franchise;"
- "Social Media Part II: Best Practices in Protecting Your Brand in the New Media;" and
- "The Awuah Case: Bellwether or Outlier."

Diana received her J.D. from Howard University School of Law and her B.A. from Georgetown University. She is a member of the American Bar Association (Forum on Franchising).

E-mail address: dvilmenay@nixonpeabody.com

Pierce Haesung Han – Pierce is an associate in Nixon Peabody's Global Business & Transactions group. Pierce focuses his practice on three main areas, assisting clients with a variety of complex business transactions.

- Mergers & Acquisitions: Providing assistance to both public and private clients with various mergers and acquisitions, performing due diligence, drafting and negotiating transaction documents, and facilitating closing and post-closing mechanics.
- International Commercial Transactions: Drafting and negotiating a variety of commercial agreements, including international franchise and development agreements, license agreements, and purchase and sale agreements.

- Federal Securities Law Matters: Assisting public and private clients regarding federal securities laws and stock exchange rules relating to corporate governance and disclosure.

Pierce serves as the Secretary of the Asian Pacific Bar Association Educational Fund (an affiliate of the Asian Pacific American Bar Association of the Greater Washington, D.C. Area).

Pierce received his J.D. from Georgetown University Law Center and his B.A. from Case Western Reserve University. He is admitted to practice in the State of New York and the District of Columbia.

E-mail address: phan@nixonpeabody.com

Keri McWilliams – Keri is an associate in the Franchise & Distribution team of Nixon Peabody LLP. Keri works with clients on a number of franchising issues, including obtaining and maintaining franchise registrations in various states, responding to state inquiries regarding trade practices, ongoing compliance with state and federal regulations, and updating franchise disclosure documents. She also handles franchise sales counseling and franchise system issues.

Keri is a member of the American Bar Association's Forum on Franchising, and the Federal and Minnesota State bar associations. She is also a member of Minnesota Women Lawyers and the Minnesota Association of Black Lawyers, and a volunteer in the Volunteer Lawyers Network.

Keri received her J.D. from Georgetown University Law Center and her B.F.A. from Washington University. She is admitted to practice in the District of Columbia and Minnesota.

E-mail address: kmcwilliams@nixonpeabody.com

Nurdin Adiwibowo – Nurdin is a partner at ABNR Law. Nurdin joined ABNR as an associate in November 2000 and became a partner on January 1, 2012. He is a law graduate of University of Indonesia majoring in Business Law. In 2000, he earned his LL.M degree in the Netherlands, majoring in International Business Law.

Prior to joining ABNR, he worked for a number of years for other prominent law firms in Jakarta. He is a registered capital market lawyer and has been involved in financing, corporate and investment projects at ABNR, and has extensive regulatory knowledge in these areas. Nurdin speaks Indonesian and English.

E-mail address: nadiwibowo@abnrlaw.com

Freddy Karyadi – Freddy is a partner at ABNR Law. Freddy joined ABNR as senior associate in July 2007 and became a partner on January 1, 2012. He studied law at University of Indonesia (1998) and Leiden University, majoring in International Tax Law (2002). He also graduated cum laude in 1997 from the Faculty of Economics of Trisakti University in Jakarta. He has participated in various trainings and seminars in Indonesia and abroad.

Prior to joining ABNR, he worked for a number of years in other prominent law firms in Jakarta. In 2010, he was seconded to Loyens & Loeffs, Amsterdam Office, a prominent Dutch law firm. His special practice areas are capital markets, M&A, taxation, banking and corporate finance matters. He has represented numerous financial institutions, banks, private equity and funds, and multinational companies.

He is a member of the editorial board of Derivatives & Financial Instruments Journal, International Bureau of Fiscal Documentation, the Netherlands and is the regional correspondence for the Indonesia jurisdiction for Tax Notes International of Virginia, United States. He also contributes articles to International Financial Law Review and a number of national tax magazines, teaches in several universities and is a regular speaker in seminars and trainings. In addition to being an advocate and tax attorney, he is also a registered accountant (Ak) and a licensed tax consultant (brevet C). Freddy speaks Indonesian and English.

E-mail address: fkaryadi@abnrlaw.com

Gustaaf Reerink – Gustaaf is a Foreign Counsel at ABNR Law. Gustaaf graduated from Leiden University in the Netherlands, where he earned an LL.M in private law, an MA in Indonesian studies, and a PhD in law, governance and development. In addition, he studied law at King's College London and the School of Oriental and African Studies in London and studied French at the University of Burgundy in Dijon. Prior to joining ABNR, he worked as an associate in the Amsterdam and Brussels offices of De Brauw Blackstone Westbroek.

His practice encompasses foreign investment, corporate, mergers & acquisitions, energy & mineral resources and related regulatory & compliance matters. He regularly publishes articles and gives presentations on Indonesian legal matters, and serves as a guest lecturer at several Indonesian universities. He is admitted to the Amsterdam

Bar and a registered foreign lawyer in Indonesia. Gustaff speaks Dutch, English, French, and Indonesian.

E-mail address: greerink@abnrlaw.com

About the Book

Franchising in Indonesia 2014: Legal and Business Considerations contains excerpts from the larger work *Franchising in Asia 2014: Legal and Business Considerations*. Both books serve as practical, succinct, easy-to-use reference tools for lawyers, business people and academics to use in navigating the laws and business issues impacting franchise arrangements in Asia.

This book provides an overview of the franchise industry in Indonesia and addresses the typical legal issues confronted when expanding a franchise system in Indonesia. The larger work, *Franchising in Asia 2014: Legal and Business Considerations*, covers those laws governing franchising in several other Asian countries.

In both books, an author, who is a legal expert in the designated jurisdiction, addresses the basic questions that a franchise lawyer would need to know to competently represent a client in expanding their franchise system to that country.

Each country chapter organizes a discussion of that country's laws under various headings and in a uniform format. Topics were sent to each country's author in the form of a questionnaire, and each author drafted responses to the questions presented. A general overview relating to the political and economic history of the country at the beginning of each chapter provides an initial context for the regulatory framework.[1]

---

[1] The source of information for these sections is the Central Intelligence Agency, https://www.cia.gov/library/publications/the-world-factbook/ (last visited May 15, 2014).

Apart from an overview of the legal framework for franchising, each book contains other articles and resources that should prove useful to those in the franchise industry.

The authors for each chapter are listed at the beginning of a chapter and their biographical information is listed in the previous section, *About the Editors and Authors.*

Readers should always consult with local counsel in the relevant jurisdiction instead of relying solely on the information contained in this book. The laws governing franchising are evolving and local counsel in Indonesia are best positioned to provide timely, relevant advice applying the current law to the particular facts of a case.

Franchising in Indonesia

Nurdin Adiwibowo, Freddy Karyadi,
and Gustaaf Reerink
ABNR Law
Jakarta, Indonesia

Indonesia

I. Introduction

A. Background

Indonesia is now the world's third most populous democracy, the world's largest archipelagic state, and the world's largest Muslim-majority nation. Since 1998, Indonesia has been developing into a modern democracy in which the rule of law is increasingly observed. Current issues include: alleviating poverty, improving education, preventing terrorism, consolidating democracy after four decades of authoritarianism, implementing economic and financial reforms, stemming corruption, reforming the criminal justice system, holding the military and police accountable for human rights violations, addressing climate change, and controlling infectious diseases, particularly those of global and regional importance. Recent reforms in the field of, among others, foreign investment law, corporate law, intellectual property law and antitrust law have contributed to Indonesia becoming an attractive country for investment. In 2005, Indonesia reached a historic peace agreement with armed separatists in Aceh, which led to democratic elections in Aceh in December 2006.

B. Economy

Indonesia, a vast polyglot nation, has grown strongly since 2010 and is the largest economy of Southeast Asia. Due to its robust annual economic growth rate of more than 6% in recent years, Indonesia recently became a member of the G-20. A major driver for Indonesia's economic success is domestic consumption, which has increased significantly as a result of an emerging consumer class. During the global financial crisis, Indonesia outperformed its regional neighbors and joined China and India as the only G-20 members posting growth. The government has promoted fiscally conservative policies, resulting in a debt-to-GDP ratio of less than 25% and historically low rates of inflation. Fitch and Moody's upgraded Indonesia's credit rating to investment grade in December 2011. Indonesia still struggles with poverty and unemployment, inadequate infrastructure, corruption, a complex regulatory environment, and unequal resource distribution among regions. The government also faces the challenges of quelling labor unrest and reducing fuel subsidies in the face of high oil prices.

The franchising sector is one of the sectors that is benefiting from recent developments. According to the Ministry of Trade, the number of domestic franchise businesses increased by 11.7% and of foreign franchise business by 6.25% in 2012. For 2013, the Ministry expects the number of domestic franchise businesses to increase by 8% and foreign franchise businesses by 14%.[2]

C. Franchise Legal Overview

Franchising in Indonesia is governed by Government Regulation No. 42 of 2007 (GR 42), which was enacted and became effective on July 23, 2007. GR 42 is implemented by Regulation of the Minister of Trade No. 53/M-DAG/PER/8/2012 dated August 24, 2012 (Regulation 53), which revoked the previous implementing regulation issued on August 21, 2008, Regulation of the Minister of Trade No. 68/M-DAG/PER/10/2012 dated October 29, 2012 (Regulation 68) and Regulation of the Minister of Trade No. 07/M-DAG/PER/2/2013 dated February 11, 2013 (Regulation 07).

The above regulations apply to franchisors and franchisees. Under these regulations, a franchisor is a private individual

[2] Bisnis Waralaba Akan Tumbuh 8-14 Persen, *Tempo*, 7 March 2013.

or a business entity that grants a right to benefit from or use a franchise that is owned by the franchisor. The franchisor can be a domestic or foreign franchisor or subsequent franchisor. A franchisee is a private individual or business entity that receives a right by the franchisor to utilize and/or use the right over the franchise owned by the franchisor. A franchisee can be a domestic or foreign franchisee or subsequent franchisee. A franchise is a special right that is owned by a private individual or a business entity in relation to a business system with distinct characteristics in marketing products or services that has been proven profitable and may be used or applied by another party on the basis of a franchising agreement.

A franchise should:

- have unique business characteristics;
- be proven profitable;
- have written standards regarding the service and the goods/services offered;
- be easy to teach and apply;
- offer continuous support;
- have registered intellectual property rights.

The Department of Trade (the DOT, formerly the Department of Trade and Industry) is the governmental agency regulating franchising. It has delegated part of its authorities to the provincial and/or regency/municipal level.

In principle, Indonesian laws and regulations have a territorial effect, which means that they (i) only regulate activities undertaken within the Indonesian territorial boundaries; (ii) can only be enforced in Indonesia; and (iii) are only applicable to entities formally established or factually doing business in Indonesia.

II. Regulatory Requirements

A. Pre-sale Disclosure

Please describe any pre-sale franchise disclosure or similar requirements that may apply to franchise transactions.

Under GR 42 and Regulation 53, there is an obligation to disclose the franchise offer prospectus and the franchise agreement to prospective franchisees no later than two weeks prior to the execution of the agreement.

The franchise offer prospectus and the franchise agreement should not only be disclosed to franchisees, but also to subsequent franchisees, which all fall under the definition of "franchisee" (see under Section I.C. above).

Although Regulation 53 does not contain any provisions relating to a transferee franchisee, it is also common practice to disclose the franchise offer prospectus and the franchise agreement to a transferee franchisee no later than two weeks prior to signing the agreement.

In practice, a franchisor is not required to disclose the franchise offer prospectus and the franchise agreement to a renewing franchisee, unless material changes to the franchise or the rights and obligations of the parties are made.

As with a franchise renewal situation, local practice suggests that the franchise offer prospectus and the franchise agreement need not be disclosed to an existing franchisee planning to execute an agreement for an additional franchise.

B. Government Approvals, Registrations, Filing Requirements

Please describe any necessary government approvals, registrations or filing requirements that may apply to franchise transactions.

GR 42 and Regulation 53 require both a franchisor and a franchisee to hold a franchise registration letter (Surat Tanda Pendaftaran Waralaba or referred to in Regulation 53 as "**STPW**") for the franchising business they are engaged in.

In order to obtain an STPW, a franchisor from abroad, a franchisor from Indonesia, a subsequent franchisor of a foreign franchise or a franchisor of a domestic franchise is required to register the franchise offer prospectus at the DOT. The franchise offer prospectus that is registered by a franchisor from abroad should be legalised by a public notary with an accompanying explanation letter from the trade attaché or an official of a representative office of the Republic of Indonesia in the franchisor's country of origin.

The franchise offer prospectus should contain information on:

- Identity of the franchisor, including a copy of the identity card of the franchisor (in case the franchisor is a private person), the identity cards of the shareholders, the members of the board of directors and the board of directors (in case the franchisor is a company (*Perseroan Terbatas* or PT));
- Legality of the franchisor business, including the trade business license (Surat Izin Usaha Dagangan or SIUP), the tourism business license (Izin tetap Usaha Pariwisata), the permit for the establishment of a

education unit (Surat Izin Pendidikan Satuan Pendidikan);

- History of business activities of the franchisor;
- Organisational structure of the franchisor;
- Financial statements of the last two years;
- Number of business units;
- Franchisees involved in the franchising business;
- Rights and obligations of the franchisor and the franchisees.

If the prosectus is written in a foreign language, it should be translated into the Indonesian language.

In order to obtain an STPW, a franchisee or a foreign franchisor is required to register the franchise agreement to which it is a party at the Department of Trade, while a franchisee of a domestic franchise, a subsequent franchisee of a foreign franchisor and a franchisee of a domestic franchisor is required to register the franchise agreement at the Trade Bureau of the Province of Jakarta Special Capital Region or the regency or municipal level or the local One Roof Services Office.

The competent authorities must issue an STPW within two business days after the submission of all required forms and documents. If the forms and documents are not complete and not in order, the competent authorities must reject the application within two business days. In practice, it takes about two to three weeks to obtain an STPW.

Before the STPW is issued, the competent authorities may request the applicant to give a presentation about the franchising activities to the Evaluation Team, which consists of the Director General of Domestic Trade and others members as needed. The evaluation by the Evaluation Team constitutes a recommendation for the approval of the issuance of the STPW.

An STPW is valid for five years and may be extended for another five years. The STPW is no longer valid upon the lapse of the validity period or the termination of the franchise agreement.

A franchisor or franchisee who fails to obtain an STPW may be imposed with an administrative sanction in the form of maximum three written warnings and a maximum Rp. 100,000,000 fine (approximately US $1,640,689.00).

A franchisor or franchisee that has already obtained an STPW is required to submit an annual report regarding the franchise activities to the DOT on March 31 of the following year at the latest.

Franchisees from Indonesia, subsequent franchisees of a foreign franchise and subsequent franchisees of a domestic franchise that have already obtained an STPW are required to submit a report regarding the franchise activities to the head of the Trade Bureau of the Province of Jakarta Special Capital Region or the regency or municipal level.

A franchisor or franchisee who fails to submit a report may be imposed with an administrative sanction in the form of a maximum of three written warnings. If following these warnings no report has been submitted, there will be a suspension of the STPW for a maximum period of two months, and if after this period if the report still has not been submitted, the STPW will be revoked.

C. Limits on Fees and Typical Term of Franchise Agreement

Please describe any limits upon the nature and extent of fees and the term of a typical franchise agreement.

According to GR 42, a franchisee agreement should contain at least the following provisions:

- Name and address of the parties;
- Type of intellectual property rights conveyed;
- Business activities;
- Rights and obligations of the parties;
- Assistance, facilities, operational guidance, supervision and marketing that will be provided by the franchisor to the franchisee;
- Business area;
- Term of the agreement;
- Manner of payment of invoices;
- Ownership, change of ownership and inheritance rights;
- Dispute resolution; and
- Method to extend, cancel and terminate the agreement.

GR 42 also puts a limit on choice of law (see under Section VII.A. below).

Apart from the above, Article 1338 of the Indonesian Civil Code recognizes the principle of freedom of contract. On the basis of this principle, parties are free to determine the content of the agreement made between them, as long as the agreement has fulfilled the requirements for an agreement to be valid as stipulated under the Article 1320 of the Indonesian Civil Code (i.e. consent of the parties, capacity of the parties to enter into an agreement, certain subjects, and permissible cause (e.g. the agreement does not contravene the prevailing regulations and principles of public order and morality)).

Courts in Indonesia may, at the request of a party to the agreement, amend or annul certain provisions of an agreement if these provisions are contrary to the principle of reasonableness and fairness.

III. Currency

If all payments under a franchise agreement must be made in immediately available U.S. Dollars, please advise as to any restrictions, reporting requirements, or regulations concerning the exchange, repatriation or remittance of U.S. Dollars.

There is no foreign exchange control in Indonesia. However, the transfer of funds in foreign currencies to and from abroad is subject to a reporting obligation to Indonesia's central bank, Bank of Indonesia. The reporting obligation is an obligation of the Indonesian party.

IV. Taxes, Tariffs, and Duties

Please do not provide any in-depth comments on tax structuring. However, please provide your general comments on the typical amount of withholding tax that would apply and whether a "gross-up" provision contained in a franchise agreement would be enforceable in your country.

Indonesian tax law imposes a withholding tax upon the royalty payable by a franchisee. If the franchisor is an Indonesian tax resident or a non-Indonesian tax resident, the rate of withholding tax is 15%. If the franchisor is a non-resident, the rate of the withholding tax is subject to whether the country where the franchisor resides or has its domicile has a tax avoidance arrangement with Indonesia. The 20% withholding tax upon the royalty paid by a franchisee is withheld if the franchisor's country does not have a double taxation arrangement with Indonesia. The relevant applicable tax treaty may reduce the withholding tax rate if the recipient can fulfil certain administrative documentation and beneficial ownership tests for passive income (in case the payment to non-resident franchisor falls under the royalty clause in the tax treaty).

In addition to the withholding tax to be paid by the franchisor, a franchisee is required to pay Value Added Tax (VAT). The standard VAT rate is 10 percent. Certain goods and services, such as food and beverages served in restaurants and catering services, are not subject to VAT. The franchisee can request the tax authorities to refund the excess of input VAT over output VAT.

If the franchisee is active in a certain industry, such as the restaurant industry, regional taxes may be imposed as well. The percentage of tax imposed may vary in each region.

As discussed under Section IV.C. above, Article 1338 of the Indonesian Civil Code recognizes the principle of freedom of contract. This also means that a gross-up provision on withholding tax contained in a franchise agreement should in principle be enforceable in Indonesia.

V. Trademarks

Please advise us as to whether there are any special requirements for granting a valid trademark license, including the use of a registered user agreement or a short trademark license agreement and any required filing of such an agreement with the trademark authorities.

According to the Indonesian Trademark Law, trademark license agreements are to be recorded at the Trademark Office. However, to date regulations implementing the law have not yet been issued. In practice, a trademark license agreement may be recorded in the Indonesia Trademark Office (ITO), which will subsequently issue a receipt of submission of the agreement. However, the ITO will not process the registration until the issuance of implementing legislation.

VI. Restrictions on Transfer

Please advise as to whether there are any restrictions (1) on a franchisor to restrict transfers by a master franchisee, any interest in a master franchisee, or the assets of the master franchisee or (2) on the ability of a master franchisee to control and/or restrict transfers of a subfranchisee's rights under a master franchise agreement, interest in the subfranchisee, or the assets of the subfranchisee.

If a franchise agreement is unilaterally terminated by the franchisor before the expiry of the agreement, the franchisor is not permitted to appoint a new franchisee for the same region before the parties have reached agreement over the settlement of disputes (clean break) or there is a binding court ruling. The DOT will not issue an STPW to the new franchisee until the clean break statement is obtained from the relevant franchisee. The clean break statement should indicate that the franchisor and the franchisee have settled all issues arising as a result of the termination. In practice, a clean break statement is also required if an existing franchisee transfers its business to a new franchisee.

VII. Termination

Please advise us as to any laws relating to termination in your country, such as agency laws, required indemnity provisions, notice or "good cause" requirements, or other laws affecting termination of a franchise agreement. Please describe.

Indonesia

As discussed under Section II.C. above, each franchise agreement should contain provisions regarding the termination of the agreement.

Under the Indonesian Civil Code, an agreement may be terminated due to incapability or a defect of consent of either of the parties at the time the agreement was entered into, a serious breach of contract, unforeseen circumstances, on the basis of the principle of reasonableness and fairness (particularly in case of indefinite agreements) or if certain conditions for termination specified in the agreement have been fulfilled.

In case none of the above circumstances apply, an agreement may only be terminated by mutual agreement between the parties.

Unless agreed otherwise between parties (by waiving Article 1266 and Article 1267 of the Indonesian Civil Code), the party wishing the agreement to be terminated should request the court to do so. If the request for termination is based on the claim of a serious breach of contract, the court has the discretionary power to set a term within which the defaulting party can remedy the breach of contract. This term should be no longer than 30 days. If parties have waived Article 1266 and Article 1267 of the Indonesian Civil Code, a party wishing to terminate the agreement, may need to give notice and set a term for the defaulting party to remedy the breach of contract.

Depending on the circumstances, either of the parties may claim damages for loss in connection with the termination of the agreement.

As discussed above, if a franchise agreement is unilaterally terminated by the franchisor before the expiry of the agreement, the franchisor is not permitted to appoint a new franchisee for the same region before the parties have reached agreement over the settlement of disputes (clean break) or there is a binding court ruling. The DOT will not issue an STPW to the new franchisee until the clean break statement is obtained from the relevant franchisee. The clean break statement should indicate that the franchisor and the franchisee have settled all issues arising as a result of the termination.

VIII. Governing Law, Jurisdiction, and Dispute Resolution

A. Choice of Law of Foreign Jurisdiction

Please confirm whether the choice of law of a foreign jurisdiction would likely to be upheld under the law of the country, except for certain matters such as trademarks, bankruptcy and competition matters, which we assume would be governed by the law in your country.

GR 42 requires that franchise arrangements are based on a franchise agreement that is governed by the laws of the Republic of Indonesia.

B. International Arbitration Dispute Resolution

Please confirm that a court in your country would honor an election of international arbitration dispute resolution, and therefore refuse to hear any disputes arising under a franchise agreement.

An election of international arbitration dispute resolution will generally be honored by the Indonesian courts. Please note:

Indonesia

(i) Any final award rendered against any of the parties in the relevant documents by an arbitration panel duly appointed and empowered in accordance with the terms of the relevant documents would be recognized and enforced against each such party by the competent courts of the Republic of Indonesia without re-examination of the merits pursuant to Law number 30 of 1999 and the 1958 New York Convention on the Recognition of and Enforcement of Foreign Arbitral Awards (the "New York Convention"). However, enforcement of an arbitral award with respect to the relevant documents against any relevant party may be denied if:

(a) the award is issued by an arbitrator or arbitration tribunal in a foreign country which is not a signatory to an international convention on the recognition of foreign arbitral awards to which Indonesia is a signatory, or does not have a bilateral arrangement with the Republic of Indonesia for the recognition of arbitral awards on a reciprocal basis,

(b) the award is not on commercial law matters, or

(c) the award is against the public policy of the Republic of Indonesia.

(ii) Indonesia is a signatory to the New York Convention and has adopted such convention into Indonesian law by way of Presidential Decree No. 34 of 1981.

The procedure for enforcement of foreign arbitral awards in Indonesia is regulated by Law number 30 of 1999 and Indonesian Supreme Court Regulation No. 1 of 1990 regarding the Procedure for the Enforcement of Foreign Arbitral Awards, which applies both to arbitral awards made in states bound by the New York Convention and to arbitral awards from States having a relevant bilateral agreement with Indonesia. In addition, to enforce the award it is necessary to register the award with the Clerk of Central Jakarta District Court, obtain a writ of execution (known as an "*Exequatur*") from the Chairman of the Central Jakarta District Court or, in case the award which involves the Republic of Indonesia as one of the parties in dispute, from the Supreme Court of the Republic of Indonesia (through the Central Jakarta District Court). With respect to this matter, however, there have been a number of instances where Indonesian Courts have refused to give effect to the enforcement of arbitration agreements or foreign arbitration awards for other specified or unspecified reasons

IX. Non-Competition Provisions

If the franchise agreement prohibits the master franchisee from engaging in certain competitive activities during the term of the agreement, and for a 12-month period after the termination or expiration of the agreement, please comment on the enforceability of non-competition covenants in your country.

In 2009, the Indonesian Commission for the Supervision of Business Supervision (Komisi Pengawasan Persaingan Usaha or KPPU) enacted Regulation of the KPPU No. 6 of 2009. The regulation provides guidelines regarding provisions that, by exemption to applicable general antitrust rules, may be used in franchise agreements and provisions that are in violation of general antitrust rules.

The principle of exemption with regard to franchise agreements is based on the idea that in principle certain provisions in franchise agreements that are essential to protect the common indentity and the reputation of the franchise network or to protect the confidentiality of intellectual property rights that are part of the franchising concept may be exempt from applicable general antitrust rules. Based on this principle, a franchise agreement may contain provisions that create certain obligations on the part of the franchisee in order to protect the franchising concept and intellectual property rights that are owned by the franchisor. Such provisions for example create an obligation on the part of the franchisee to use a business method that is determined by the franchisor, a prohibition to change the franchising location without informing the franchisor or the prohibition to share information regarding intellectual property rights with third parties, even after the expiry of the franchising agreement.

In principle, a limitation of business activities by the franchisor within an agreed area and a limitation of business activities of the franchisee within this area is also permissable. However, this may not result in an absolute protection of the area of sales, for instance by directly or indirectly hindering customers to obtain products or services for the reason that they reside outside the agreed area and effectively dividing the market. In other words, a limitation of the area in which the franchisee may undertake business activities that is not created to form a franchise network but instead is meant to limit the market and customers is in violation with antitrust rules.

Provisions in franchise agreements regarding the obligation to obtain certain products from the franchisor or a certain third party are usually meant to protect the quality standard of franchise products. This protection of the miminum quality of products is important in a franchise business to uphold the identity of the franchising concept itself. However, the obligation to obtain certain products is not permissable if it does not relate to products that are essential to the franchise concept. Equally, a franchisor may not prohibit a franchisee to acquire products and/or services from third parties which products and/or services fulfill the quality standards determined by the franchisor.

Franchise agreements commonly contain provisions that aim to maintain resale prices. These provisions are usually meant to prevent franchisees from selling their products at a price that would harm the franchise identity/image. According to the guidelines, a recommended (and thus non-binding) resale price would be permissable. However, provisions regarding resale prices that would lead to a price cartel, so that there can be no competition on price would be in violation with antitrust rules.

Provisions that oblige franchisees to acquire various sorts of products from the franchisor to guarantee the quality standard of the franchising concept would not be contradictory to business competition principles. However, such an obligation may limit product substitution and thus hinder competition. Therefore, an obligation for the franchisee to acquire products that are not related to the franchise concept, creating an entry barrier for other enterpreneurs, is not permissable.

Provisions that prohibit franchisees to undertake business activities that could compete with the franchise business network can be justified. Such an prohibition is usually meant to protect the intellectual property rights of the franchisor and guarantee the identity and reputation of the franchise network, particularly if the franchisor has already transferred certain knowhow. However, the long term hindering of competing business activities may hinder competition and technological progress, thus, negatively influencing economic efficiency. Therefore, provisions that prohibit franchisees to undertake equal business activities for a long period after the expiry of the franchise agreement should be avoided. In determining the term which does not limit business competition, the KPPU will take various aspects into consideration, including the franchise technology, the investments made and the nature of the franchise products. If the franchise technology is already part of the public domain, the term that competing business activities may not be undertaken by franchisees is usually one year.

The guidelines explicitly state that franchise agreements containing provisions which may hinder or put a limit on franchisees in doing business, potentially resulting in a monopoly or unhealthy business competition, are not exempt from applicable general antitrust rules. This means that franchise agreements containing provisions that lead to price fixing, limitation of supplies, tying of franchise products with products outside the franchising concept, market division, and non-competition clauses that remain applicable after the expiry of the agreement are potentially in violation with general antitrust principles.

X. Language Requirements

Does the law in your country require that a franchise agreement be translated into the local language in order to be enforceable between the parties?

In accordance with GR 42, if a franchise agreement is written in a foreign language, the agreement must be translated into the Indonesian language or risk being deemed invalid.

XI. Other Significant Matters

Please advise as to whether there are any significant matters not addressed above of which a franchisor should be aware in connection with its entering into a franchise agreement in your country.

Regulation 53 and in particular Regulations 68 and 7 contain provisions that aim to support and protect local small and medium enterprises.

Regulation 53 requires a franchisor and franchisee to use raw materials, business equipment and sell products that are at least 80% domestically produced. In certain cases, the DOT may give permission, upon recommendation by the Evaluation Team, to use raw materials, business equipment and sell products that are less than 80% domestically produced.

The same regulation also requires a franchisor to give support to the franchisee in the form of education and training in the management of the franchisee, regular guidance in operational management, support in developing business through promotion (advertising, leaflets/catalogues/brochures or exhibitions) and research on and development of business and products that can be traded.

A franchisor or franchisee who fails to use raw materials, business equipment and sell products that are at least 80% domestically produced or a franchisor who fails to give support to the franchisee may be imposed with an administrative sanction in the form of a maximum of three written warnings. If following these warnings no report has been submitted, the STPW will be suspended for a maximum period of two months, and if after this period still no report has been submitted, the STPW will be revoked.

Finally, the regulation requires a franchisor to cooperate with local small and medium entrepreneurs in the local area as franchisees or goods/service suppliers as long as they meet the requirements set by the franchisor. Regulation 53 does not stipulate what will be the sanction if a franchisor fails to meet this requirement.

Regulation 68 creates specific obligations for franchisors and franchisees that own outlets of so-called Modern Shops. A Modern Shop is a shop with an independent service system, which sells various types of retail products, for instance minimarkets, supermarkets, department stores, hypermarkets or wholesale grocery stores. Most importantly, Regulation 68 limits the number of outlets of so-called Modern Shops that may owned by franchisors and franchisees to 150. In the event the franchisors or franchisees owns 150 outlets and want to open more outlets, at least 40% of these extra outlets should be franchised to local small and medium business partners. This obligation only applies to Modern Shops of, in case of mini markets, less than 400 m², in case of supermarkets, less than 1,200 m², and in case of department stores, less than 2,000 m². Furthermore, this obligation does not apply to franchisors and franchisees (i) who have not yet made any profit, as evidenced by financial statements audited by a registered accountant, (ii) following an evaluation by the Evaluation Team, are deemed to be unable to find a local business partner who can become a franchisee.

Franchisors and franchisees must meet the above obligation within five years after the enactment of the regulation (so before October 29, 2017) by each year releasing at least 20% of the outlets that are required to be franchised by the franchisor or franchisee.

The Regulation creates obligations similar to those based on Regulation 53, namely that franchisor should sell products that are at least 80% domestically produced and is required to give support to the franchisee in the form of training and guidance in the management and in meeting services standards and quality of products that are being traded. The same sanctions may be imposed as those which may be imposed on the basis of Regulation 53.

Regulation 7 creates specific obligations for franchisors and franchisees that own food and beverage outlets, such as restaurants, bars and cafes. Most importantly, Regulation 68 limits the number of food and beverages outlets that may be owned franchisors and franchisees to 250. In the event the franchisors or franchisees owns 250 outlets and want to open more outlets, these extra outlets should be franchised or a collaboration with capital participation should be entered into. If franchisors or franchisees opt for a collaboration with capital participation, the other party should invest, in case of an investment of Rp 10 billion or less, at least 40% and in case of an investment of more than Rp. 10 billion, at least 30%. Priority should be given to franchising to or entering into a collaboration with local small or medium business partners.

Franchisors and franchisees must meet the above obligation within five years after the enactment of the regulation (so before February 14, 2018).

Regulation 7 creates obligations similar to those based on Regulations 53 and 68, namely that franchisors and franchisees should use raw materials and business equipment that are at least 80% domestically produced. In certain cases, the DOT may give permission, upon recommendation by the Evaluation Team, to use raw materials, business equipment and sell products that are less than 80% domestically produced. Furthermore, franchisors are required to give support to the franchisee in the form of training and guidance in the management and in meeting services standards and quality of products that are being traded. The same sanctions may be imposed as those which may be imposed on the basis of Regulations 53 and 68.

Bibliography of International Franchise Resources

Kendal H. Tyre, Jr., Diana Vilmenay-Hammond, Pierce Haesung Han and Keri McWilliams
Nixon Peabody LLP
Washington, D.C.

I. General International Resources

Mark Abell, Gary R. Duvall, and Andrea Oricchio Kirsh, *International Franchise Legislation* B1, ABA FORUM ON FRANCHISING (1996)

Kathleen C. Anderson and Anthony M. Stiegler, *Put Muscle in Your Marks: Enforcing Intellectual Property Rights* W14, ABA FORUM ON FRANCHISING (1995)

Richard M. Asbill and Jane W. LaFranchi, *International Franchise Sales Laws—A Survey* W7, ABA FORUM ON FRANCHISING (2005)

Jeffery A. Brimer, Alison C. McElroy, and John Pratt, *Going International: What Additional Restraints Will You Face?* W4, ABA FORUM ON FRANCHISING (2011)

Michael G. Brennan, Alexander Konigsberg, and Philip F. Zeidman, *Globetrotting: A Workshop on International Franchising* 10/W8, ABA FORUM ON FRANCHISING (1994)

Michael G. Brennan, Alexander Konigsberg, and Philip F. Zeidman, *Globetrotting: Strategies for Launching U.S.*

Franchisors Abroad 2/P2, ABA FORUM ON FRANCHISING (1994)

Christopher P. Bussert and Jennifer Dolman, *Regaining Your Trademark After Abandonment or Misappropriation* W7, ABA FORUM ON FRANCHISING (2011)

Ronald T. Coleman and Linda K. Stevens, *Trade Secrets and Confidential Information: Rights and Remedies* W2, ABA FORUM ON FRANCHISING (2000)

Finola Cunningham, *Commerce Department Helps Franchisors Go Global*, in FRANCHISING WORLD 63 (Dec. 2005)

Michael R. Daigle and Alex S. Konigsberg, *Meeting Off-Shore Disclosure and Contract Requirements* F/W13, ABA FORUM ON FRANCHISING (1992)

Jennifer Dolman, Robert A. Lauer, and Lawrence M. Weinberg, Structuring International Master Franchise Relationships for Success and Responding When Things Go Awry W22, ABA FORUM ON FRANCHISING (2007)

Gary R. Duvall, Paul Jones, and Jane LaFranchi, *Planning for the International Enforcement of Franchise Agreements* W6, ABA FORUM ON FRANCHISING (1999)

William Edwards, International Expansion: Do Opportunities Outweigh Challenges? in FRANCHISING WORLD (February 2008)

George J. Eydt and Stuart Hershman, *Bringing a Foreign Franchise System to the United States* W9, ABA FORUM ON FRANCHISING (2009)

William A. Finkelstein and Louis T. Pirkey, *International Trademarks* W15, ABA FORUM ON FRANCHISING (1991)

William A. Finkelstein, Protecting Trademarks Internationally: Current Strategies and Developments B3, ABA FORUM ON FRANCHISING (1996)

Stephen Giles, Lou H. Jones, and Lawrence Weinberg, *Negotiating and Documenting Complex International Franchise Agreements* W21, ABA FORUM ON FRANCHISING (2006)

Steven M. Goldman, Stephen Giles, Marc Israel, and Stanley Wong, *Competition Round Up from Around the World* LB2, ABA FORUM ON FRANCHISING (2004)

David C. Gryce and E. Lynn Perry, *Trademarks and Copyrights in the International Arena* 6/W4, ABA FORUM ON FRANCHISING (1993)

Kenneth S. Kaplan, Andrew P. Loewinger, and Penelope J. Ward, *System Standards in International Franchising* W14, ABA FORUM ON FRANCHISING (2005)

Edward Levitt and Jorge Mondragon, A Survey of International Legal Traps and How to Avoid Them—Beyond the Franchise Laws W20, ABA FORUM ON FRANCHISING (2007)

Ned Levitt, Kendal H. Tyre, and Penny Ward, *The Impossible Dream: Controlling Your International Franchise System* W4, ABA FORUM ON FRANCHISING (2010)

Michael K. Lindsey and Andrew P. Loewinger, *International (Non-U.S.) Franchise Disclosure Requirements* W9, ABA FORUM ON FRANCHISING (2002)

Andrew P. Loewinger and John Pratt, *Recent Changes and Trends in International Franchise Laws* W4, ABA FORUM ON FRANCHISING (2008)

Andrew P. Loewinger and Thomas M. Pitegoff, Avoiding the Long Arm of the Law in International Franchising: Issues and Approaches W8, ABA FORUM ON FRANCHISING (1995)

Craig J. Madson and Katherine C. Spelman, *Similarity and Confusion in the Intellectual Property Arena* W11, ABA FORUM ON FRANCHISING (1997)

Christopher A. Nowak, John Pratt, and Carl E. Zwisler, *Franchising Internationally with Countries with Opaque Legal Systems* W20, ABA FORUM ON FRANCHISING (2006)

E. Lynn Perry and John L. Sullivan Jr., *Trademark Compliance and Enforcement Techniques* E/W12, ABA FORUM ON FRANCHISING (1992)

Marcel Portmann, *Franchising Sector Proves Global Reach*, in FRANCHISING WORLD (January 2007)

John Pratt and Luiz Henrique O. do Amaral, Civil Law for Common Law Practitioners (or How to Draft an Agreement for Use Overseas) W4, ABA FORUM ON FRANCHISING (2002)

Kirk W. Reilly, Robert F. Salkowski and Geoffrey B. Shaw, *Determining the Rules of Engagement in Litigation Here and Abroad* W5, ABA FORUM ON FRANCHISING (2008)

Catherine Riesterer and Frank Zaid, *Basics of International Franchising* L/B2, ABA FORUM ON FRANCHISING (1997)

W. Andrew Scott and Christopher N. Wormald, *Stranger in a Strange Land: Contrasting Franchising in International Expansion* W2, ABA FORUM ON FRANCHISING (2003)

Donald Smith and Erik Wulff, *International Franchising: The Unraveling of an International Franchise Relationship* 15/W13, ABA FORUM ON FRANCHISING (1993)

Frank Zaid, Pamela Mills, and Michael Santa Maria, *Essential Issues in International Franchising* LB/1, ABA FORUM ON FRANCHISING (2001)

II. Asian Resources

Stephen Giles, Andrew P. Loewinger, and Sherin Sakr, *Go East Young Franchisor: Franchising in Asia-Pacific Other Than China and India* W21, ABA FORUM ON FRANCHISING (2011)

Stephen Giles, *Franchising in Asia-Pacific Region, Who's Who Legal*: FRANCHISE 2012 (2012)

A. China

Ren Yanling, *Changes to Chinese Franchise Law: An improved Balance Between the Interests of Franchisors and Franchisees*, in INT'L JOURNAL OF FRANCHISING LAW 3 (2012)

China: New Franchising Law, in Int'l Journal of FRANCHISING LAW 2 (2005)

Ella S.K. Cheong, *China*, in INTERNATIONAL FRANCHISING CHN/1 (Dennis Campbell gen. ed. 2011)

Yu Qin and Richard L. Wageman, *China*, in INTERNATIONAL FRANCHISE SALES LAWS China-1 (Andrew P. Loewinger and Michael K. Lindsey eds. 2010)

Mark Abell, Daniela C. Brito, and Paul D. Jones, *Franchising in the BRIC Markets (Brazil, Russia, India, and China)* W18, ABA FORUM ON FRANCHISING (2008)

B. Hong Kong

Andrea S.Y. Fong, *Hong Kong*, in INTERNATIONAL FRANCHISING HK/1 (Dennis Campbell gen. ed. 2011)

C. India

Preeti Mehta, *India—Termination of Master Franchise Agreements and the Consequences*, in INT'L JOURNAL OF FRANCHISING LAW 3 (2007)

Yoginder Pal, *Franchising in India*, FRANCHISING WORLD (October 2006)

Mark Abell, Daniela C. Brito and Paul D. Jones, *Franchising in the BRIC Markets (Brazil, Russia, India, and China)* W18, ABA FORUM ON FRANCHISING (2008)

D. Indonesia

Sigit Ardianto and Rivan F. Ramadhan, *Indonesia*, in INTERNATIONAL FRANCHISING INA/1 (Dennis Campbell gen. ed. 2011)

Rick Beckman and Ferry P. Madian, *Indonesia*, in INTERNATIONAL FRANCHISE SALES LAWS Indonesia-1 (Andrew P. Loewinger and Michael K. Lindsey eds. 2010)

Kendal H. Tyre, Jr. & Pierce Haesung Han, *The Ministry of Trade of Indonesia Limits Growth of Food and Beverage Franchises*, NIXON PEABODY LLP: FRANCHISE ALERT (February 2013)

E. Japan

Takenari Shimizu, *Japan*, in INTERNATIONAL FRANCHISING JAP/1 (Dennis Campbell gen. ed. 2011)

Souichirou Kozuka and Takashi Kanai, *Japan*, in INTERNATIONAL FRANCHISE SALES LAWS Japan-1 (Andrew P. Loewinger and Michael K. Lindsey eds. 2010)

F. Malaysia

Leela Baskaran, *Malaysia*, in INTERNATIONAL FRANCHISING MAY/1 (Dennis Campbell gen. ed. 2011)

Mohd Bustaman Hj Abdullah and Wong Sai Fong, *Malaysia*, in INTERNATIONAL FRANCHISE SALES LAWS Malaysia-1 (Andrew P. Loewinger and Michael K. Lindsey eds. 2010)

Kendal H. Tyre, Jr. & Pierce Haesung Han, *Malaysian Government Actively Promotes Growth in Franchise Sector*, NIXON PEABODY LLP: FRANCHISE ALERT (October 2013)

Kendal H. Tyre, Jr. & Pierce Haesung Han, *Tapping Into Malaysia's Aggressive Franchising Goals*, PORTFOLIO MEDIA, INC.: LAW360 (November 2013)

G. Singapore

Daniel Lim, Bernard Lui, Michele The, and Vanessa Chew, *Singapore*, in INTERNATIONAL FRANCHISING SIN/1 (Dennis Campbell gen. ed. 2011)

H. South Korea

Brendon Carr and Jae-Hoon Kim, *South Korea*, in INTERNATIONAL FRANCHISE SALES LAWS South Korea-1 (Andrew P. Loewinger and Michael K. Lindsey eds. 2010)

Kendal H. Tyre, Jr. & Pierce Haesung Han, *South Korea adopts major amendments to the Fair Transactions in Franchise Business Act*, NIXON PEABODY LLP: FRANCHISE LAW ALERT (January 2014)

I. Taiwan

Wellington Liu and David Lu, *Taiwan*, in INTERNATIONAL FRANCHISE SALES LAWS Taiwan-1 (Andrew P. Loewinger and Michael K. Lindsey eds. 2010)

J. Thailand

Alan Adcock and Sriwan Puapondh, *Thailand*, in INTERNATIONAL FRANCHISING THA/1 (Dennis Campbell gen. ed. 2011)

K. Vietnam

Mai Minh Hang and Nguyen Anh Tran, *Vietnam*, in INTERNATIONAL FRANCHISE SALES LAWS Vietnam-1 (Andrew P. Loewinger and Michael K. Lindsey eds. 2010)

Printed in Dunstable, United Kingdom

91342625R00030